D0604675

THE STORY OF THE UNITED STATES

A NATION IS BORN:
1754-1820s

by Lois Sepahban

Content Consultant
Stuart Leibiger
Associate Professor of History
Salle University

CORE
LIBRARY

Published by ABDO Publishing Company, PO Box 398166, Minneapolis, MN 55439. Copyright © 2014 by Abdo Consulting Group, Inc. International copyrights reserved in all countries. No part of this book may be reproduced in any form without written permission from the publisher. The Core Library™ is a trademark and logo of ABDO Publishing Company.

Printed in the United States of America, North Mankato, Minnesota
092013
012014

Editor: Jenna Gleisner
Series Designer: Becky Daum

Library of Congress Control Number: 2013945665

Cataloging-in-Publication Data
Sepahban, Lois.
 A nation is born: 1754-1820s / Lois Sepahban.
   p. cm. -- (The story of the United States)
Includes bibliographical references and index.
ISBN 978-1-62403-173-1
1. United States--History--Revolution, 1775-1783--Juvenile literature. 2. United States--Social life and customs--To 1820--Juvenile literature. I. Title.
973.3--dc23

                                              2013945665

Photo Credits: North Wind Picture Archives/AP Images, cover, 1; Washington and Lee University, 4; Red Line Editorial, 7, 31; North Wind/ North Wind Picture Archives, 8, 15, 18, 23, 32, 36, 38; National Portrait Gallery, London, 10; John Singleton Copley, 13; Architect of the Capitol, 21, 45; Howard Chandler Christy, 26; The Frick Collection, New York, 29

Cover: An argument between colonists and British soldiers escalates into the Boston Massacre on March 5, 1770, resulting in five dead colonists.

CONTENTS

CHAPTER ONE
The French and Indian War 4

CHAPTER TWO
Seeds of Revolution 10

CHAPTER THREE
War! 18

CHAPTER FOUR
A New Nation 26

CHAPTER FIVE
War and Westward
Expansion 32

Important Dates. 42

Stop and Think 44

Glossary. 46

Learn More. 47

Index 48

About the Author 48

THE FRENCH AND INDIAN WAR

On January 16, 1754, Major George Washington arrived in Williamsburg, Virginia. He had just finished an approximately 900-mile (1,448-km) mission for Governor Robert Dinwiddie of Virginia. The weather had been bad along the way. Many of the horses were weighed down and slow in the snow. Washington had to leave behind his horse and many

George Washington was involved in politics long before becoming the first US president.

of his men. He carried his belongings and walked much of the way. He was only 21 years old.

Washington's important mission was to deliver letters to the French leader in the Ohio River Valley. The letters were from the governor. They said the lands in the Ohio River Valley belonged to the British. They asked the French soldiers to leave the forts they had built there and return to Canada. The French refused to leave.

Fort Duquesne

In 1754 the French took over and claimed Fort Duquesne. The fort sat where Pittsburgh, Pennsylvania, is located today. In the spring, Governor Dinwiddie sent Washington to this fort to speak to the French. This time no friendly letters were exchanged. Instead, Washington's small military force met French forces. In the battle on July 4, 1754, Washington was defeated and surrendered. The French and Indian War had begun.

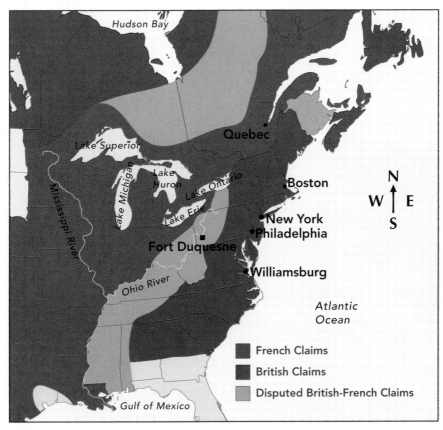

North America in 1754

Look at the map showing how North America was divided in 1754. The British said the land in the Ohio River Valley belonged to them. The French said the land was theirs. In 1754 this disagreement became a war. How does the information on the map help you better understand the reasons for the French and Indian War?

American Colonists and the War

For the British and the French, the French and Indian War was a fight about which country was the most powerful in the world. Their fight took place

George Washington and his men attack French forces during the French and Indian War.

in Europe, India, the West Indies, and in the North American colonies. The French had many Native-American allies. The British had almost none. The French and their Native American allies began attacking colonists living on the frontier. The colonists began to fight back.

Slaves Join the War

At the same time, African-American men joined the fight. Some were free, but many were slaves. Slavery was common in North America at the time. Slaves were usually men, women, and children who had been taken from Africa and sold as slaves in North America. Others were born in North America to African slaves. Many slaves fought in the French and Indian War. They hoped to earn their freedom by fighting.

The French were defeated at Fort Duquesne in 1758 and again in the siege of Quebec in 1759. In 1763 the British and the French signed the Treaty of Paris. The war was over. The French lost all of their land in North America to the British. The British Empire became the largest in the world. And the colonists learned they could unite to defeat a common enemy.

The Treaty of Paris

The British and French signed the Treaty of Paris in 1763. Because the French lost the war, they gave up all of their land in North America. Canada and all of the land east of the Mississippi River went to the British. New Orleans and all of the land west of the Mississippi River went to the Spanish.

CHAPTER TWO

SEEDS OF REVOLUTION

After the war the British had to make peace with the Native Americans. King George III of Great Britain did this with the Royal Proclamation of 1763. This proclamation told colonists they could not build settlements west of the Appalachian Mountains. They had to leave this land for Native Americans.

The British controlled the 13 American colonies: New Hampshire, Massachusetts, Rhode Island,

King George III ruled Great Britain and Ireland from 1760 to 1820.

Connecticut, New York, Pennsylvania, New Jersey, Delaware, Maryland, Virginia, North Carolina, South Carolina, and Georgia. Life in the colonies depended on farms. The farms needed land. Some colonists had already moved west for more farmland. They lived on the frontier. Many more colonists wanted to join them. They were upset by King George III's proclamation.

The Stamp Act of 1765

King George III also angered those living in towns and cities. He taxed the colonists on everyday items, such as sugar and tea. Another act, called the Stamp Act, taxed documents printed on paper. The colonists said the king and his Parliament, the group elected to make laws in Great Britain, couldn't tax them unless they agreed. The colonists had no representatives in Parliament. They argued this made the taxes illegal.

The Sons of Liberty

Samuel Adams formed the Sons of Liberty in 1765. This group was made up of colonists living in Boston,

Samuel Adams founded the Sons of Liberty, a group that greatly opposed British rule in the colonies.

Massachusetts. They rioted and protested taxes. They attacked tax collectors. They burned official buildings and documents. As a result Great Britain sent British soldiers to Boston starting in 1768. These British soldiers were unpopular. Newspaper articles described how they harmed colonists.

The Boston Massacre

On the night of March 5, 1770, the anger the colonists felt for the British soldiers reached a dangerous point. An argument between the colonists and British soldiers turned into violence. Colonists threw rocks at a group of British soldiers. Eventually the soldiers fired their guns. Five colonists died. News of the Boston Massacre spread across the 13 colonies.

The Boston Tea Party

The British continued to issue acts to control the colonists and gain money. The Tea Act of 1773 told colonists they could only buy tea from the East India Tea Company. The colonists thought this was unfair. When ships from the East India Tea Company sailed into Boston Harbor, the people of Boston would not let them unload the tea. They said the ships must leave. The East India Tea Company refused. On December 16, 1773, a mob of Bostonians boarded the ships. Some of the people were disguised as Mohawk

Boston men disguised as Mohawk Native Americans destroyed chests of tea and dumped them in the Boston Harbor as an act of protest against the Tea Act of 1773.

Native Americans. They dumped 347 chests of tea into the water.

The Coercive Acts

King George III decided to punish the colonists and try to restore order with the Coercive Acts of 1774. These acts closed the Boston port. They also

The Committees of Correspondence

The Coercive Acts greatly angered the colonists. They joined together to form their own emergency governments. These were called Committees of Correspondence. Members communicated with one another. But they did not report to King George III or Parliament. During this time, communicating over such a large area was difficult. Members of the committees wrote articles for newspapers, sent letters, and gave speeches. They used spies to find out what the British soldiers were doing.

forced the colonists to let soldiers stay in their homes. In addition, the colonists in Massachusetts lost the right to choose its own colonial government. All government officials had to show they were loyal to King George III.

The Continental Congress

Representatives from all colonies met in Philadelphia, Pennsylvania, on September 5, 1774. They discussed Parliament's taxes. The meeting was called the First Continental Congress. Many famous colonists were sent by their colonies to be representatives. George Washington and Patrick Henry represented Virginia. John Adams and Samuel Adams represented Massachusetts.

The representatives made a list of the rights every citizen should have. They called it the Declaration and Resolves of the First Continental Congress. They said the colonists had the right to life, liberty, and property. They said keeping the British army in the colonies was illegal. They agreed to meet again the following May.

EXPLORE ONLINE

The Web site below has more information about the Boston Massacre and what really happened that night. As you know, every source is different. How is the information on the Web site different from the information in this chapter? What information is the same? How do the two sources present information differently? What can you learn from this Web site?

The Boston Massacre
www.mycorelibrary.com/a-nation-is-born

CHAPTER THREE

WAR!

By spring 1775, colonists were fed up with Parliament's laws. They were ready to fight. They had weapons stored in Concord, Massachusetts. On the night of April 18, 1775, the Boston Committee of Correspondence sent colonist Paul Revere to Lexington, Massachusetts, to warn Samuel Adams and John Hancock that British troops were coming to arrest them.

On his ride to Lexington, Massachusetts, Paul Revere warned people that the British were coming.

Minutemen

In the months before the first shots were fired in Lexington, colonists began to prepare for war. Farmers and tradesmen secretly trained to fight British soldiers. They collected weapons and ammunition. They formed militias. These militias included soldiers called "minutemen." They could be ready to fight at a minute's notice.

Lexington, Massachusetts, was on the path to Concord. The people of Lexington heard the alarm. Men and boys gathered with whatever weapons they had. When the British soldiers arrived, they ordered the Lexington militia to put their weapons down. The militia refused. The leader of the militia told his men to leave. But before they could, someone fired a shot. British soldiers then shot into the crowd, leaving eight men dead and nine others wounded. Nobody is certain who fired that first shot, but it was a shot that changed the world. The American Revolution, the war between Great Britain and the American colonies, had begun.

Thomas Jefferson and other drafters of the Declaration present the Declaration of Independence to Congress.

The Second Continental Congress

Almost a month later, on May 10, 1775, representatives met in Philadelphia for the Second Continental Congress. They discussed the battles in Lexington and Concord. They appointed George Washington to be the general of the Continental Army. The army was made up of colonists who wanted to fight against the British soldiers. The Congress nominated Thomas Jefferson to lead the writing of the Declaration of Independence. The Declaration claimed the colonies' independence from Great Britain. The Congress approved the Declaration on July 4, 1776.

The Battles of Saratoga

In the meantime war continued. The British military was larger and better equipped than the Continental Army. Washington's soldiers were often hungry. Few had warm coats and shoes for winter. They were not trained soldiers. It looked as though the British would win.

Then in the fall of 1777, the Continental Army defeated the British near Saratoga, New York. Within a year, the French also declared war on Great Britain. They sided with the Americans.

British general John Burgoyne surrenders to Continental Army general Horatio Gates at the Battle of Saratoga.

The End of the War

The Continental Congress had little money. It could not pay soldiers or buy them food, clothes, or shoes. Soldiers often left the army to work on their farms or spend time with their families. Many soldiers died during the winter from sickness and hunger. But the Continental Army still fought. Washington's soldiers and their French allies trapped the British army in Yorktown, Virginia. On October 19, 1781, British general Charles Cornwallis surrendered.

After eight years of war, the Americans and the British signed the Treaty of Paris in 1783. With the signing, war was finally over. The British army and navy left. Great Britain still owned Canada, but the 13 colonies were now free and independent. They were now the United States of America.

In 1776 the Continental Congress asked Thomas Jefferson to write the Declaration of Independence, claiming freedom from Great Britain:

> We . . . the Representatives of the united States of America . . . solemnly publish and declare, That these United Colonies are, and of Right ought to be Free and Independent States; that they are Absolved from all Allegiance to the British Crown, and that all political connection between them and the State of Great Britain, is and ought to be totally dissolved. . . . And for the support of this Declaration, . . . we mutually pledge to each other our Lives, our Fortunes, and our sacred Honor.

Source: "Declaration of Independence." The Charters of Freedom. *National Archives*, n.d. Web. Accessed May 15, 2013.

Consider Your Audience

Read this passage carefully. Jefferson wrote the Declaration of Independence for his fellow adults. Rewrite this passage for a young audience. How does the vocabulary of your Declaration of Independence differ from the original text and why?

CHAPTER FOUR

A NEW NATION

With the Revolutionary War over, each state worried another state would grow stronger. In 1777 Congress had adopted the Articles of Confederation, the first set of laws governing the United States. The Articles of Confederation created a new government in which each state held more power than one central government. The government was not strong, but it kept the states working together.

Washington led the Constitutional Convention in Philadelphia, where representatives from the states met to draft the US Constitution.

The Constitution

The Continental Congress had very little power. Leaders of the Continental Congress, such as George Washington and James Madison, thought the country needed a stronger central government. On May 25, 1787, representatives from most of the states met in Philadelphia.

The meeting lasted four months. Representatives argued about whether a central government should have more power than the states. They argued about whether or not slavery should be legal. At the end of the meeting, they had written the Constitution. This document set up the basic laws that would govern the new nation.

Representatives took the Constitution back to their states to vote on it. Some states did not want to accept the Constitution right away. So the Bill of Rights was created. These were ten amendments, or additional laws, that protected citizens' rights. These rights included freedom of speech, freedom

President Washington set an example, showing that political power could pass from one president to another peacefully.

to choose your own religion, freedom to write and publish newspapers, and freedom to meet in peaceful groups. By 1791 all of the original 13 states voted to ratify, or accept, the Constitution.

A New Government

The first election for president was on January 7, 1789. George Washington won. During the eight years he was president, Washington chose the first Supreme Court, chose a cabinet, or group of advisors, and signed a law to set up the first national bank. John Adams became the second president

Our Nation's Capital

Washington, DC, was not always the capital of the United States. In 1790 Philadelphia was named as the temporary capital. The Continental Congress and the Constitutional Convention both met there. Before John and Abigail Adams moved into the White House in 1800, the United States Congress met in New York City.

in 1797. Thomas Jefferson became the third president in 1801.

The Louisiana Purchase

In 1803 President Jefferson purchased the Louisiana Territory from France for $15 million. The Louisiana Territory was an area of approximately 828,000 square miles (1,332,537 sq km). It stretched from the Mississippi River in the east to the Rocky Mountains in the West. This land doubled the size of the United States. Most of the land west of the Mississippi River was unexplored. So in 1804 President Jefferson sent Meriwether Lewis and William Clark on an expedition to explore the new land. Their goal was to find an all-water route to the Pacific Ocean.

The Lewis and Clark Expedition

Meriwether Lewis and William Clark led an expedition to the Pacific Ocean from 1804 to 1805. Look at the map showing their route. Imagine you are on the expedition. Think about some of the dangers you might face. Write a journal entry describing your experience.

Lewis and Clark began their expedition in May 1804 in Saint Louis, Missouri. After traveling by land and water, they reached the Pacific on November 15, 1805. They never found an all-water route because it does not exist. But they did bring back information about the West. This inspired many settlers to move west.

CHAPTER FIVE

WAR AND WESTWARD EXPANSION

By the time James Madison became president in 1809, Great Britain and France were at war. The United States was neutral, meaning the states did not pick a side. But Great Britain and France ignored those wishes. They stopped US trade with European countries, stealing US ships and cargo. They even kidnapped US sailors and forced them to join the British navy.

Great Britain halted US trade by blocking off Atlantic Ocean waterways, such as the Chesapeake Bay, sparking the War of 1812.

War with Native Americans

Many Native-American tribes became allies with Great Britain during the War of 1812. These tribes were angry with the United States for taking their land. Led by Tecumseh, a Shawnee chief, the tribes fought against US troops. When Tecumseh was killed in battle in 1813, most of the tribes stopped fighting.

Another War with Great Britain

In 1812 Congress declared war on Great Britain. US troops attacked Canada, which was a colony of Great Britain. The stronger British army defeated the Americans. Soon after, the US troops surrendered Fort Detroit in the Michigan Territory.

An End to the War

The war went back and forth. In 1814 the Treaty of Ghent officially ended the war. US victories on land and at sea forced the British to officially honor US boundaries. Americans proved they could survive a war. US trade grew stronger as Britain stopped stealing US ships and cargo. The United States now had time to address other problems.

Expanding West

When James Monroe became president in 1817, the United States was growing. Many Americans wanted to move west. But Native-American tribes already occupied the land in the West. The US government forced the Native Americans to sign treaties. These treaties said Native Americans had to give up their land to the settlers and move to new land.

The settlers who moved west wanted the territory they lived on to become states. In 1819 Missouri asked to join the United States as a

Andrew Jackson

Andrew Jackson was a major general in the US Army during the War of 1812. He defeated the Creek Indians, who were allies of Great Britain in 1814. He became a war hero after he defeated the British in the Battle of New Orleans on January 8, 1815. Jackson was so popular that he became president in 1829.

Fighting often broke out between settlers moving west and Native Americans who already inhabited western land.

slave state. That meant people in Missouri could own slaves.

Slavery in the New Nation

Before the American Revolution, it was legal to own slaves in all colonies. Slowly the northern states began to make slavery illegal. Southern farmers kept large plantations. They needed many workers to tend to them. These workers were African-American slaves. Southern plantation owners claimed that without slaves they couldn't run their plantations.

The Missouri Compromise

If Missouri became a state, there would be

Slavery

The system of slavery that existed in the South was very harsh. Slaves were the property of their owners. Slave families were often forced apart. African-American children were often taken from their parents and sold away. Slaves who attempted to run away were beaten or killed.

Slaves on southern plantations were forced to work in fields from sunrise to sunset.

more slave states than free states. Slavery was illegal in the northern states. It was legal in the southern slave states.

The states reached a compromise in 1820 when Maine asked to join the United States as a free state. The Missouri Compromise of 1820 drew an imaginary line across the United States. It applied to the Louisiana Purchase territory west of the Mississippi River. Free states were north of the line, and slave states were south of it. Missouri finally became a slave state in 1821.

The Monroe Doctrine

In 1823 President Monroe issued a message called the Monroe Doctrine. This doctrine encouraged the act of keeping out of other countries' business. It said European countries could not form new colonies in North and South America. It also stated European countries could not get involved in the politics of North and South America. If they did, the United States would consider it an act of war.

Conflicts to Come

Arguments over slavery separated the free states in the North and slave states in the South. As the nation grew westward, settlers and Native Americans had more conflicts. The Missouri Compromise and treaties with the Native Americans solved these problems for a short time. But the United States was still growing, and these issues would come up again.

On September 13, 1814, Francis Scott Key watched the British bomb Baltimore, Maryland. The next morning, he could see that the US flag still flew over Fort McHenry. He was inspired to write "The Star-Spangled Banner":

> O say can you see by the dawn's early light,
>
> What so proudly we hailed at the twilight's last gleaming,
>
> Whose broad stripes and bright stars through the perilous fight,
>
> O'er the ramparts we watched, were so gallantly streaming?
>
> And the rockets' red glare, the bombs bursting in air,
>
> Gave proof through the night that our flag was still there;
>
> O say does that star-spangled banner yet wave,
>
> O'er the land of the free and the home of the brave?

Source: Francis Scott Key. "The Star-Spangled Banner." Smithsonian. Smithsonian National Museum of American History, n.d. Web. Accessed May 17, 2013.

What's the Big Idea?

Take a close look at the passage. What is the author saying about his feelings as he watched the bombing of Fort McHenry during the night? What is he saying about his feelings when he saw that the flag still flew over the fort?

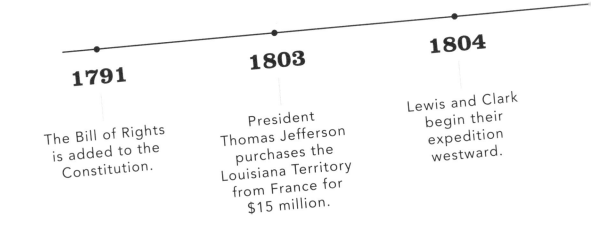

1754

The French and Indian War begins between Great Britain and France.

1763

The French and British sign the Treaty of Paris to end the French and Indian War.

1775

The American Revolution begins between Great Britain and the American colonies on the night of April 18.

1791

The Bill of Rights is added to the Constitution.

1803

President Thomas Jefferson purchases the Louisiana Territory from France for $15 million.

1804

Lewis and Clark begin their expedition westward.

1776

The Declaration of Independence is approved on July 4.

1783

The Americans and British sign the Treaty of Paris to end the American Revolution.

1789

George Washington is elected the first president of the United States on January 7.

1812

The War of 1812 begins between Great Britain and the United States.

1814

The Americans and British sign the Treaty of Ghent to end the War of 1812.

1823

President James Monroe announces the Monroe Doctrine to Congress. It declares all of North and South America off limits to European countries.

STOP AND THINK

Say What?

Studying US history can mean learning a lot of new vocabulary. Find five words in this book you have never seen or heard before. Use a dictionary to find out what each word means. Then rewrite the meanings in your own words and use each word in a new sentence.

Why Do I Care?

The American Revolution ended more than 200 years ago. But you can still find similarities between your life and the world of the early colonists. How might your life be different if colonists had never settled in North America? Use examples from this book to explain how the early colonists helped shape the United States.

Surprise Me

Chapter Five discusses the War of 1812. After reading this book, what two or three facts about the War of 1812 did you find the most surprising? Write a few sentences about each fact. Why did you find them surprising?

Tell the Tale

Chapter Four discusses the Lewis and Clark expedition. Write 200 words that tell the story of their journey. What did they watch for? What might they have worried about? Be sure to set the scene, develop a sequence of events, and write a conclusion.

GLOSSARY

compromise
an agreement between people with opposite views in which each side gives up some demands

expedition
a journey taken for a specific purpose

frontier
the far edge of an area where not many people live

independence
freedom from outside control or support

massacre
the cruel and violent killing of many people

Parliament
the group of people elected to make laws in Great Britain

riot
to create or join in public violence or disorder

surrender
to give up or hand something over

treaty
a written agreement between two countries

LEARN MORE

Books

Metz, Lorijo. *The American Revolution*. New York: PowerKids Press, 2014.

Rissman, Rebecca. *The Declaration of Independence*. Minneapolis: ABDO, 2013.

Schmidt, Maegan. *The US Constitution and Bill of Rights*. Minneapolis: ABDO, 2013.

Web Links

To learn more about the American Revolution, visit ABDO Publishing Company online at **www.abdopublishing.com**. Web sites about the American Revolution are featured on our Book Links page. These links are routinely monitored and updated to provide the most current information available.

Visit **www.mycorelibrary.com** for free additional tools for teachers and students.

INDEX

Adams, John, 17, 29
Adams, Samuel, 12, 17, 19
American Revolution, 19–24
Articles of Confederation, 27

Bill of Rights, 28
Boston Massacre, 14
Boston Tea Party, 14–15

Clark, William, 30–31
Committees of Correspondence, 16, 19
Constitution, 28–29
Continental Army, 21, 22, 23–24
Continental Congress, 16–17, 21, 23, 25, 28, 30

Declaration of Independence, 21–22, 25

Fort Duquesne, 6, 9
French and Indian War, 6–9

George III (king), 11, 12, 15, 16

Jackson, Andrew, 35
Jefferson, Thomas, 21, 25, 30

Lewis, Meriwether, 30–31
Louisiana Purchase, 30, 39

Madison, James, 28, 33

Missouri Compromise, 37, 39, 40
Monroe, James, 35, 39
Monroe Doctrine, 39

Native Americans, 8, 11, 15, 34, 35, 40

Parliament, 12, 16, 19

slaves, 8–9, 22, 37
Stamp Act, 12

Tea Act, 14
Tecumseh, 34
Treaty of Ghent, 34
Treaty of Paris, 9, 24

War of 1812, 34–35
Washington, George, 5–6, 16, 21, 22, 23, 28, 29

ABOUT THE AUTHOR

Lois Sepahban has taught every grade from kindergarten to high school. She once drove through the Columbia River Gorge, imagining she was a member of the Lewis and Clark Expedition. She likes to read, write, and rescue animals.